CONTACT
CAPITAL

How to turn your contacts into cashflow

BOB PROCTOR

Contact Capital
How to Turn Your Contacts into Cashflow

Printed in the United States of America

ISBN: 10: 1-891279-25-4

Published by INTI, Inc.
Cover design and layout by Parry Design Studio

intipublishing.com

Classic Image Illustrates the Power of Touch

The image on the front cover is a rendering of one of the most famous and copied artworks in history—a close-up from Michelangelo's painting on the ceiling of the Sistine Chapel depicting God giving Adam the spark of life.

Although completed nearly 500 years ago, Michelangelo's iconic image still strikes a chord with viewers today because it reminds us of a modern-day truth—that technology is a *supplement to*, not a *substitute for* our most valuable asset, our relationships. *Technology*, no matter how pervasive or sophisticated, can never take the place of *touch-nology*.

As I write in this book, "There's no replacement for human touch.

"You can't digitize a hug or a handshake.

"You can't e-mail eye contact.

"You can't text message a touch."

This book is about getting back in touch with touch. Touching people will do wonders for your business life. Your personal life. And your soul.

Dedication

This book is dedicated to every business owner and entrepreneur who is developing the understanding of how to turn contacts into capital.

Acknowledgments

I would like to acknowledge a series of mentors who led me to the information that literally changed my life. These are the people who helped me to understand that contacts, without question, are the most valuable capital that you will ever encounter.

Ray Stanford put *Think and Grow Rich* in my hands, and through reading that book, I began to think for the first time in my life. Up until that point, I was merely a human instrument that was being directed by people, activities, conditions and circumstances. Napoleon Hill woke me up to the value of goals, masterminding and seeking guidance from people who demonstrated by results, that they knew what they were doing.

That book led me to Earl Nightingale's recordings and ultimately to the Nightingale-Conant Corporation. Earl Nightingale and Lloyd Conant became two extremely important people in my life. Earl taught me how to study, what to study and how to take what I had learned and put it into action. And it was Lloyd Conant who taught me the value of building relationships; he was a master at it. It was Lloyd and Earl who instilled in me a desire that has only grown stronger over the years—a desire to teach to others the information that impacted my life so greatly.

It was through the Nightingale-Conant Corporation that I met a truly wise man, Leland Val Van De Wall, who, in turn, introduced me to one of his mentors, Dr. C. Harry Roder. Together, they took me on a journey into the depths of the mind and taught me things that only a few people ever learn during the course of their lives. The essence of what they taught me has formed the foundation for all of the programs I have taught around the world for the past 40 years. It was also at the Nightingale-Conant Corporation that I met and became friends with a man whom I had listened to for a number of years. He was better known as the "Frank Sinatra of Public Speakers," Mr. Bill Gove. Bill was the man who taught me how to perfect the skill of public speaking. He was a wonderful friend and a great mentor.

These were the people who truly helped me develop an understanding that has led me to a very rich and rewarding life. Hopefully, you will catch the essence of some of what I have learned in the following few pages.

Contents

Economists are struggling to measure the intangible assets of human-capital development. What exactly is their added value to the business?

—*from Business: The Ultimate Resource*

What Is Capital and How Is It Changing?

What job pays $30,000 a year for daytime work and upwards of $30 million a year for work during evenings and weekends?

Answer: English teacher... that is, if you happen to be Stephen King, author of many horror classics, including *Carrie* and *The Shining*.

King started out his career teaching high school English in the state of Maine. But it wasn't his talents as a teacher that made him one of the richest people in the entertainment industry. It was his talent as a writer of spellbinding novels that have sold hundreds of millions of copies worldwide and been adapted into movies, video games, and dozens of spin-off products that keep the cash registers ringing.

Creative Capital

What enabled a low-paid teacher to transform himself into a mega-millionaire is a concept I call **creative capital**. Before moving on, let's look at this word **capital** for a moment. We see and hear the word **capital** all the time, mostly in regard to the stock market and world economy.

Here are a few of the variations of the word I came across one morning in the daily newspaper.

Capital markets.

Capitalize.

Capital investments.

Capital expenditure.

Capital goods.

Working capital.

Capital-gains tax.

Capitalism.

The word **capital** gets used a lot is because it's the cornerstone of the free market system. Although the concept is powerful, the definition is very simple.

Here's *Webster's* definition:

cap·i·tal *n. Wealth, in any form, used to create more wealth.*

When most people talk about **capital**, they're referring to **tangible capital**, such as real estate, stocks and bonds, gold, manufacturing facilities, and, most commonly, money.

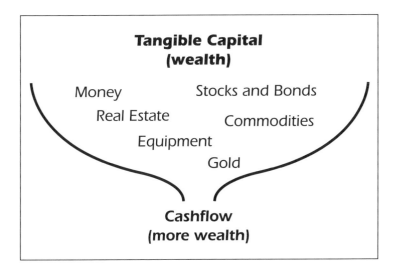

But in this book, we're going to be talking about **contact capital**, an **intangible capital** that you can convert into cashflow. In a nutshell, your **contact capital** consists of people you know personally or people you're connected to through a community, such as a club, church, school, etc. The beauty of **contact capital** is that everyone has it in abundance, but few people recognize its huge potential as a profit center.

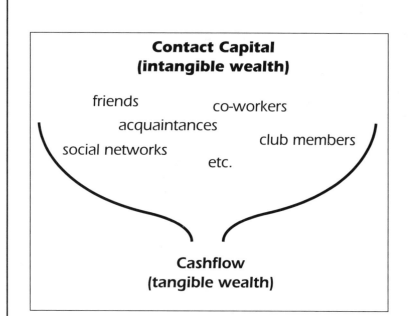

Leverage Your Contacts, Live Your Dreams

After reading this book, you'll understand how you can leverage your contacts to live your dreams by creating financial freedom... and time freedom... for yourself and your family.

So, let's get started learning how to turn contacts into cashflow.

Turn to the next chapter to learn how **capital** is changing from a rare commodity controlled by a few super-lucky people from super-rich families... to an abundant commodity controlled by ordinary individuals like you and me.

The individual is the central, rarest, most precious capital resource of our society.
—*Peter Drucker,*
management guru

2

Tangible vs. Intangible Capital: And the Winner Is...?

Let's review the definition of capital:

Capital: *Wealth, in any form, used to create more wealth.*

Let's look at how this definition might work for both **tangible** and **intangible assets**. First, let's look at a typical scenario involving **tangible capital** that happens thousands of times a day all over the world.

A Tale of Tangible Capital

Rick the Retiree decides to put his capital to work without incurring much risk. He invests $10,000 in a one-year CD paying 5%. At the end of 12 months, his CD would have grown to $10,500.

Putting Tangible Capital to Work

Tangible capital investment

$10,000 @ 5% simple interest

Capital Gains = $500

Rick the Retiree is a classic example of a person putting his **tangible capital** to work.

But take another look at the first part of the definition of **capital**—"*Wealth, in any form, to create more wealth.*" In the first chapter we saw how Stephen King used his "wealth in any form" (which, in his case, was a wealth of writing talent) to earn hundreds of millions of dollars. True, few people are blessed with King's **creative capital,** but today, the world is rife with other types of **intangible capital** that have only recently become available, thanks to the growth of capital markets and modern technology.

Here are a few other types of **intangible capital** receiving recognition and endorsements from business analysts and marketing consultants:

Types of Intangible Capital

Human capital: The accumulated skills, knowledge, experience, capabilities, and wisdom of a company's owners and employees.

Spiritual capital: A company or person who acts in accordance with integrity, vision, meaning, purpose, and positive values while seeking to earn a profit.

Customer capital: The value of relationships with customers, suppliers, allies, and partners.

Intellectual capital: Content, patents, copyrights, trademarks, etc. owned by a company or individual

e-Capital: Ability to translate a concept into a profitable Web-supported or Web-based business.

From Intangible Capital to Tangible Cash

A perfect example of newly available **intangible capital** is Internet domain names. In the early 1990s, when the Internet was just getting started, Mark Ostrovsky speculated that companies would pay tons of money for domain names with key words in the title. So he registered dozens of "can't miss" domain names, such as *Business.com*, with the sole purpose of selling them to the highest bidder.

His strategy worked. He sold *Business.com* for $7.5 million and *Autos.com* for $2.2 million. Ironically, Ostrovsky refers to domain names as "real estate," but unlike the real estate in the Old Economy, the real estate in the New Economy is more likely to be digital than dirt.

Many Different Kinds of Intangible Capital

Coca-Cola is a great example of another lucrative type of **intangible capital** known as **brand capital**. *BusinessWeek* magazine estimates that Coca-Cola's **brand capital**, that is, the power of the Coca-Cola name and reputation to generate new business, is worth about $6.5 billion PER YEAR, making it the top brand in the world.

Earning billions a year just because of the power of your name—that's big-time **brand capital**, wouldn't you agree?

Intangible Capital—the New Heavyweight Champion

The value of capital was already shifting from **tangible capital** to **intangible capital** by the time the Internet came along, but the Internet supercharged the process.

It took General Electric and Exxon Mobil, for example, 100 years and billions of dollars of **tangible capital** investments (factories, warehouses, refineries, machinery, raw materials, inventory, etc.) to reach a market capitalization of $150 billion.

It took Google *less than three years to create the same amount of investor wealth* using relatively little **tangible capital** (tens of thousands of servers and computers linked together) and loads of **intangible capital** in the form of digitized information, brilliant founders and employees, and a razzle-dazzle brand name.

Google and Coca Cola are just two examples of the growing impact of **intangible capital** on the world economy. As our world becomes more digital… more global… and more interconnected each day, **intangible capital** will continue to overtake **tangible capital** in both influence and income.

New Economy = New Rules

Old Economy Tangible Capital Ruled	**New Economy** Intangible Capital Rules
money, land, buildings, offices, manufacturing, equipment, inventory, etc.	**contacts, creativity, intellect, brand name, reputation, innovation, e-capital, etc.**

To understand the evolution of capital and how the transition from **tangible capital** to **intangible capital** is changing your world (and why you need to redefine the way you think about your work and the way wealth is created), turn to the next chapter.

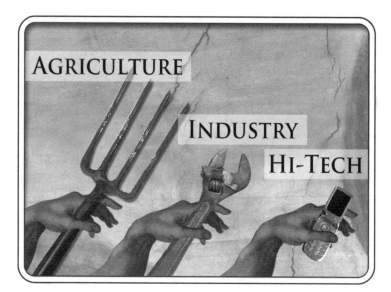

Change is the law of life. And those who look only to the past or present are certain to miss the future.

—*John F. Kennedy*

3

The e-volution of Capitalism 3.0

As I write this, wages for average workers in the U.S. are going down, yet retail sales keep going up.

What gives? I can answer that question in one word.

China.

Since Chairman Mao's death, China has reversed course and is embracing capitalism in a furious race to catch up with the prosperity of the West. The plan is working, big time. Today, China manufactures 50% of everything the world consumes.

How did China become manufacturer to the world in only two decades, and what does it bode for YOUR economic future? Before I answer that, first, a brief history lesson.

A Crash Course in Capitalism

Capitalism, as we know it today, has only been around since 1776, the year of two world-changing events—the American Revolution and the publication of Adam Smith's seminal book, *The Wealth of Nations*.

The American Revolution launched democracy.

Adam Smith launched capitalism.

The Founding Fathers despised the economic system England forced upon the colonists. The colonists rightly objected to an economic system rigged to favor England.

Negative Impact of Colonialism on America

Heavy taxes   Stiff Tariffs   Few freedoms

State-sponsored businesses

Adam Smith suggested a form of commerce that was just as radical as the U.S. Constitution. Smith argued that people will act in their own best interest in buying and selling goods and services, which should be encouraged. Smith's ideas ushered in modern-day free enterprise.

Adam Smith's Views of Capitalism

Low taxes   Private businesses
                Free Trade
Small government   Right to own land
              More freedoms for masses

The Founding Fathers adopted Smith's theory, and **Capitalism 1.0** was born. Over the next 230 years, capitalism evolved from **Capitalism 1.0** in the 18th and 19th centuries… to **Capitalism 2.0** in the mid-20th century… to **Capitalism 3.0** today. Let's take a brief look at each stage.

Capitalism 1.0

Agriculture and the Industrial Revolution dominated the American economy from the early 1600s until the late 1800s, a period when the U.S. blossomed from a struggling colony of England to a legitimate world power.
Capitalism 1.0 culminated in the Gilded Age, a time when a few giant industrialists and robber barons controlled 90% of the wealth while 80% of population worked 10-hour days as low-paid laborers.

Capitalism 2.0

Manufacturing took a big leap forward in the early 1900s with the advent of the assembly line pioneered by Henry Ford. World War II cranked up the manufacturing sector, and well-paying manufacturing jobs remained plentiful after the war as the economy prospered. But the biggest shift in the economy occurred in the 1950s, when, for the first time in history, white-collar jobs outnumbered blue-collar jobs as the Information Age powered into overdrive while automation started whittling away at manufacturing jobs.

Capitalism 3.0

In 1992, the U.S. Congress voted to commercialize the Internet, and in less than a decade, the World Wide Web ushered in a **Capitalism 3.0**, a digitized globally linked, instant-access world of commerce and communication that is changing the world at warp speed. Meanwhile, major corporations began outsourcing jobs and driving down wages. Easy access to free information on the Web is forcing centuries-old industries, such as daily newspapers, to re-invent their business models or go the way of the horse and buggy.

Why We Can't Compete with China

So, what does the e-volution of capitalism from **Capitalism 1.0** to **Capitalism 3.0** mean to you? It means the once secure, well-paying **Capitalism 2.0** jobs are being eliminated, and of those jobs that remain, salaries are being slashed.

Compare today's salaries to those of 1972:

1972 Salaries	2007 Salaries
Salary for male employee with a high school diploma	Salary for average manufacturing worker today
$42,000	**$29,000**
(in today's money)	

During the last 35 years, while the world economy was booming, average salaries for U.S. workers *dropped 31%, a loss of more than $1,000 a month*! If that's not bad enough, the costs for all basics—food, rent, transportation, and healthcare—have all grown faster than inflation.

North American factory workers, who currently earn an average of $21 an hour, are trying to compete with Chinese workers, who earn *an average of $0.64 an hour*! When it's 30 times cheaper to manufacture in China than the U.S., it's not hard to figure out why American manufacturers are fleeing to China, is it?

I tell you, it's scary out there—and getting scarier.

White-collar jobs aren't doing any better than blue-collar jobs. A few decades ago, a college degree would almost guarantee a nice, secure middle management job with perks and a pension.

Not anymore.

Capitalism 3.0, ushered in by the Internet, changed all that. Sure, a few super-smart techies loaded with **intellectual capital** are striking it rich on the Internet. But those people are one in a million.

Odds are you aren't one of them.

Contact Capital to the Rescue

What happens to average people, like you and me? What kind of capital do we have that we can leverage into a profitable business in **Capitalism 3.0**?

The answer: **contact capital**.

You see, we may not have the technical talents to flourish in **Capitalism 3.0**, but we do have contacts. And in **Capitalism 3.0**, where the cold, hi-tech Internet is rewriting the rule book, people will seek the warmth of hi-touch contacts. And the more hi-tech the world becomes, the most people will seek hi-touch experiences and encounters.

Which is why **contact capital**, more than **intellectual capital** or **financial capital** or any other capital, will become the coin of the realm in the years ahead.

Facebook.com and other social networking sites are alloys, bonding together the Internet and the real world.

—*Newsweek*

4

Facebook.com vs. Face-to-Face

Imagine you're a 19-year-old college freshman, and between classes, you start an Internet social networking Website. Now imagine that three years later, when you're only 22, Google offers you $1 billion to buy your site.

Would you turn it down? Not likely.

But Mark Zuckerberg did just that because he thought his brainchild, *Facebook.com*, was worth a lot more than a billion. A year after Google's offer, it looks like Zuckerberg was right— *Forbes* magazine estimates *Facebook* is worth $7 to $10 billion in 2007… and possibly much more in the years ahead.

From a bright idea to $10 billion in three years. Boggles the mind, doesn't it?

Zuckerberg is just one more example of how lucrative **intellectual capital** has become in **Capitalism 3.0**, the Age of the Internet. But in Zuckerberg's case, the thing that makes his **intellectual capital** so valuable is the oldest, most basic kind of capital of all—**contact capital**.

Contacting and Communicating in Cyberspace

Zuckerberg calls *Facebook* a "social graph," which is an online network of real life connections that enables users to communicate with friends, family, co-workers, and community members.

Originally restricted to just college students, today *Facebook* is open to anyone older than 13. Of the 250,000 new members who sign up daily, the majority are 25 or older—a trend that Zuckerberg predicts will continue as more and more working adults seek a way to contact and communicate with people they know or would like to know.

What is a social networking site and what makes *Facebook* so special that it's adding a million new people a week? Social networking is cyberspace's version of a local hangout or a break room at work.

Things to Do On Facebook.com

Chat   Share stories   Set appointments

Make presentations   Gossip

Swap photos and videos   Make new friends

In short, *Facebook* is an easy-to-use communication facilitator, and because the site earns money on banner ads and sponsorships, it's free to users.

Don't Mistake Facebook for Face-to-Face

Social networking sites like *Facebook* serve a valuable purpose. They enable us to enrich our connections with people currently in our social grid and allow us to expand our circle of contacts.

Because we're now operating in **Capitalism 3.0**, *Facebook* and other social networking sites (such as the high-income *aSmallWorld.net* and business-oriented *LinkedIn.com*) raise the value and amount of our **contact capital**.

So far, so good.

But be forewarned—when it comes to **contact capital**, *Facebook* can never replace face-to-face. To paraphrase John Naisbitt's observation in his benchmark bestseller, *Megatrends*:

> **The more hi-tech we have, the more counter balancing hi-touch we need.**
> —**John Naisbitt**
> *Megatrends* **Author**

No matter how sophisticated an online facilitator is, in the end, there's no substitute for human touch.

You can't digitize a hug or a handshake.

You can't e-mail eye contact.

You can't text-message a touch.

In our personal lives, there are dozens of occasions when nothing can take the place of a personal appearance. We're expected to be present during joyous celebrations, such as weddings, graduations, birthdays, holidays, and family reunions, as well as memorable milestones and solemn occasions, such as retirements, tributes, or funerals.

Same goes for our business lives—nothing, and I mean NOTHING—can take the place of face-to-face when it comes to important business protocols, such as making a presentation... managing people... courting a new client... teaching and training new people... closing a deal... or participating in a regional or national conference.

Sure, hi-tech devices are great, but by their very nature they're soulless, which is why they'll never replace the energy of a live event... the passion of a great live presentation or performance... or the feeling you get when you connect face-to-face with another human being in mind and spirit.

'No E-mail Fridays'

Corporations are just now beginning to acknowledge that face-to-face communication is far superior to e-communication. A growing number of giant employers, including U.S. Cellular, Deloitte & Touche, and Intel, are imposing "no e-mail Fridays or weekends."

The e-mail bans do not extend to urgent matters but are aimed at getting employees to strengthen relationships and increase productivity by talking with co-workers and clients face-to-face or over the phone.

The "no e-mail" movement stemmed from managers noting that employees were passing issues back and forth in long message strings via e-mail, instead of settling the issues and moving on. To complicate matters, terse and poorly worded messages were being misinterpreted, further straining relationships.

By banning e-mail, managers and workers are using Fridays to drop in for face-to-face visits, helping them to restore relationships and unplug communication bottlenecks.

"Business isn't only about e-mailing each other cold reports," says Kathy Volpi, a marketing director for U.S. Cellular. "It's about human beings and interaction."

These days, even the most modern, hi-tech companies are recognizing that hi-touch is an inborn human need that will never go out of style.

Why Touch Means So Much

Humans don't just *want* touch—they *need* touch. Studies show that children who were seldom touched and cuddled as infants are stunted intellectually and emotionally, often for all of their lives.

Even as adults, we never outgrow our inborn need to be touched physically and emotionally. That's why we must fight the temptation to take the easy way out and use hi-tech to replace hi-touch.

Today, it's easy to "reach out and touch someone" electronically through a phone call or e-mail. But the flip side is that the *e-world* makes it even easier to withdraw from the *real world*. Getting the most out of your **contact capital** means using hi-tech tools to arrange hi-touch meetings.

You've likely heard the expression, "The medium is the message," which means the *method of communication* is as important—and often MORE important—than the message itself. When you e-mail someone, the *hi-tech medium of e-mail* says, "I'm thinking of you." But when you show up in person, the *hi-touch medium of face-to-face* says, "I care about you and honor our relationship."

Big difference in messages, wouldn't you say?

Statistics Drive Home the Point

The strongest argument for face-to-face communication is not what we say with our words when we talk, but what we say with our tone of voice and body language.

Research shows that only 7% of our communication is conveyed by our words. An additional 38% is conveyed by our tone of voice. And a massive 55% is communicated non-verbally by way of our dress, appearance, facial expressions, and body language. *Which means a staggering 93% of our communication is non-verbal.*

So, to maximize your **contact capital**, you have to "be" a lot of things:

Be sincere.

Be professional.

Be confident.

Be yourself.

But above all, BE THERE IN PERSON!

Do that, and your **contact capital** will pay huge dividends down the road.

Entrepreneurs are the forgotten heroes of America.

—*President Ronald Reagan*

5

Welcome to the Age of the Entrepreneur

The U.S. is by far the world's largest economy, despite having only 4% of the world's population.

Why?

Because we're a nation of entrepreneurs!

Our entrepreneurial roots go back 400 years to 1607, when English investors hoping to discover gold in the New World founded Jamestown, Virginia.

The backers of Jamestown ended up losing their shirts, but unbeknownst to them, they accidentally planted the seeds for modern-day capitalism. To recruit more colonists and raise more capital, the London-based Virginia Company started giving settlers parcels of land, and, as an added incentive, they allowed them to vote.

Jamestown Experiment

Three Basic Rights Plant the Seeds of Free Enterprise & Entrepreneurship

1. Right to own land
2. Right to own businesses
3. Right to vote

Entrepreneurship in Our DNA

Over the centuries, North America has attracted entrepreneurs like filings to a magnet because only the boldest and the brightest would risk their lives and spend their last dime to travel thousands of miles over storm-tossed oceans to seek opportunity in a foreign land.

Just imagine spending your life savings to move to a foreign country, unable to speak the language, unfamiliar with the customs, unemployed, but driven by the dream of someday owning your own business and shaping your own destiny—that's the ultimate entrepreneur, wouldn't you say?

Between 1892 and 1930, almost 12 million of these immigrants were processed through Ellis Island in New York Harbor, the largest voluntary migration in history.

Ellis Island Immigrant Groups (1892-1930)

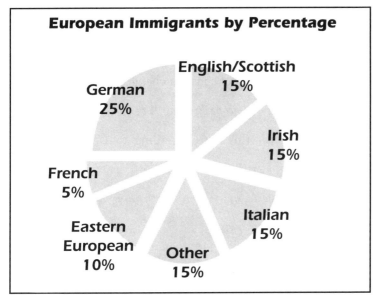

European Immigrants by Percentage

German 25%

English/Scottish 15%

Irish 15%

French 5%

Italian 15%

Eastern European 10%

Other 15%

More than 100 million U.S. citizens are descended from the wave of immigrants who passed through Ellis Island, which means you or your spouse's DNA is likely stamped with the same entrepreneurial traits as your ancestors'. Recent surveys prove this to be true. North Americans open businesses at twice the rate of the British and four times the rate of Western Europeans.

Entrepreneurship on the Rise

Today, more and more people are tapping into their entrepreneurial roots and opening businesses in record numbers, reasoning that in an era of constant change and massive layoffs *it's riskier to work for someone else than to be self-employed.*

The facts bear this out: According to *USA Today*, one out of every eight Americans age 17 to 65 is trying to start a business—that calculates to *20 million working-age people* setting up businesses of their own.

The U.S. is not the only country enjoying a sudden surge of entrepreneurship—it's a worldwide phenomenon, fanned by the fall of communism in Russia and fueled by China's state-controlled version of capitalism.

Where there are free people and free markets, there you will find entrepreneurship taking root and spreading its branches.

Welcome to the Age of the Entrepreneur.

What Opportunities Are Entrepreneurs Seeking Most?

There are dozens of reasons people choose to release their inner entrepreneurs. Here is a list of the top 10 opportunities that motivate people to go into business for themselves:

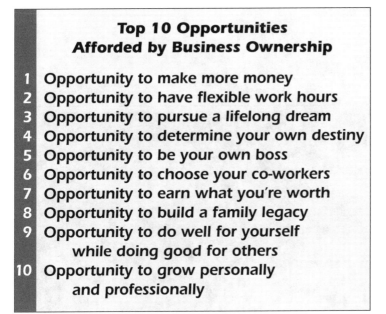

Which of these opportunities resonates most with you?

Although "Opportunity to make more money" is first on this list, making more money may be last on your personal list. But that's the best part of owning your own business—you start it and run it for YOUR REASONS, not someone else's reasons.

To find out which business gives you the *highest potential return on* **contact capital** *with the smallest outlay of* **financial capital,** turn to the next chapter.

The modern direct selling industry is poised to become the distribution method of choice for all new products and services.

—*Paul Zane Pilzer*
The Next Millionaires

6

Referral Marketing: The Best Vehicle for Converting Contact Capital into Cashflow

For tens of millions of people around the globe, the burning question isn't, "Should I open a business of my own?"

Rather, the question is, *"What kind of business should I open?"*

People looking to open their own business have basically three choices:

1) Start-up business

2) Franchise

3) **Referral marketing**, a.k.a., affiliate marketing or network marketing.

The biggest drawback for the first two types of businesses—start-ups and franchises—is that they require a workable business plan and substantial **financial capital** to get up and running.

Let's take a brief look at the options.

Advantage of Franchising

The biggest advantage of franchising is the proven, connect-the-dots business model, which helps new franchisees avoid costly missteps. Franchising takes the guess work out of operating a business, but successful franchises come at a price—a *steep price.*

The typical franchising fee is $20,000 to $35,000, which just gives the franchisee the right to open a single location. But don't close the checkbook just yet—the big expenses are just starting! It will cost tens of thousands more (or in many cases, hundreds of thousands more) to lease space... purchase equipment... stock inventory... train employees... and buy insurance BEFORE your first customer even steps foot in the door. On top of that, you'll pay the franchisor 10% of gross income for royalties and marketing fees.

Oh, you'll need plenty of **working capital** to pay your bills until the revenue stream covers your overhead, which commonly takes two to three years.

Referral Marketing to the Rescue

Franchising—great concept, but it's too expensive for the average person. What if there were a business that took advantage the two biggest benefits of franchising—independent business ownership combined with a proven, copy-cat marketing plan that virtually anyone can follow—without the huge upfront fees and massive monthly overhead to keep you awake at night?

That would be an ideal business, wouldn't it?

That would be **referral marketing**.

The beauty of **referral marketing** is that it comes so naturally to us. If you see a great movie or eat at a great restaurant, the next day you recommend it to your friends and acquaintances, right? Word-of-mouth is the best and most effective form of advertising ever invented.

Ironically, the movie studios and restaurants, along with dozens of other businesses, are making millions on the **contact capital** that we eagerly give away for free.

If they're making money on our contacts, why shouldn't we?

Referral marketing turns your contacts into cashflow by paying you for purchases made by your referrals of products and services that you use and enjoy and feel passionate about. Since you're recommending products or services that your contacts want and need anyway, why not help yourself while helping others improve and enhance their lives both physically and financially?

Major Businesses Rely on Referrals

Many prominent industries have long relied on referrals to boost business. Consultants… business brokers… mortgage companies… fine art dealers… and dozens of other enterprises use referrals as a way to find new clients and expand their businesses.

Banks and investment brokerages uniformly pay employees for recommending the company's services to friends and acquaintances. IBM Global Financing generously rewards clients for steering new business to IBM's lending division. And in the real estate industry, agents are routinely compensated for referring their clients to home inspectors, attorneys, appraisers, lenders, and title companies.

First-hand Experience with Referrals

As a professional speaker and trainer, I've had firsthand experience with referrals for more than 40 years. Most of my talks are booked through my office or website, but a sizable number of bookings come from independent brokers or "speakers' bureaus."

These bureaus have contacts with dozens of speakers and oftentimes, hundreds of companies and organizations. When a company needs a speaker, they'll call a speakers' bureau for a recommendation. For recommending the talent and booking the event, the bureau receives a commission, thereby turning their contacts into cashflow.

Again, everybody wins in this arrangement: The speaker gets paid for speaking on a date that would otherwise be open. The organization gets a qualified speaker. And the speakers' bureau earns a commission for putting the two parties together.

It's a win/win all around.

Today's Referral Marketing Is Exponential

A great thing about making money on referral sales is that it doesn't require a fancy office or a lot of expensive, sophisticated equipment. All it requires is a cell phone and Internet access.

Best of all, referrals are perfectly suited to **Capitalism 3.0**, as referrals primarily leverage **contact capital**, which everyone has in abundance, as opposed to **intellectual capital** or **financial**

capital, which are scarce, hard-to-come-by assets possessed by a fortunate few.

The downside of most referral and/or affiliate programs is that they are **linear**, meaning they *improve by addition*. To earn 10 commissions, for example, you'd have to initiate 10 successful transactions between the seller and the buyer.

A **linear growth** chart would look like this:

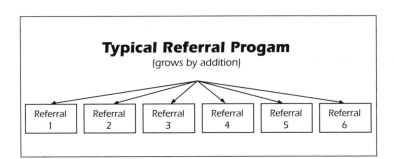

But today's **referral marketing** takes referrals to a whole new level—no, make that *whole new levels*—of compensation. **Referral marketing** empowers you to build a referral network by recruiting others and then teaching and training them to do the same, thereby giving you the opportunity to grow your business **exponentially** by multiplication. An **exponential growth** chart would look like this:

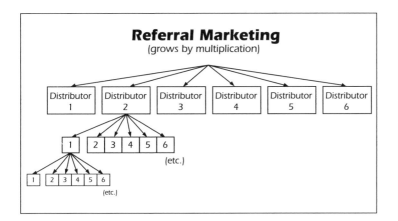

Referral Marketing: Making Money with Your Friends

Just think—instead of working at a job where you trade your time for money and having to start from zero every workday morning, with **referral marketing**, you can leverage your efforts, enabling you to build an ongoing income stream based on a percentage of the referrals from your entire organization.

That's what I call, "working smarter, not harder."

The most common objection to **referral marketing** comes from people saying, "I don't want to make money on my friends."

Personally, I'd rather do business with people I know and trust than take a chance with strangers.

Truth is, your contacts are going to buy things they want and need from somebody—which means someone, somewhere, is going to turn your contacts into cashflow—so why shouldn't that "someone" be you?

Besides, in **referral marketing**, you don't make money *from* your friends—you make money *with* your friends while helping them live their dreams, which doesn't happen when your contacts shop at Target or Wal-Mart or hundreds of other retailers they buy from, does it?

There's never been a better time for people to tap into their **contact capital** than today, right now. And there has never been a better concept to grow a business **exponentially** and turn contacts into cashflow than **referral marketing**, a $100-billion-a-year industry that has enjoyed growth for 20 consecutive years, and, according to experts, "the next 10 years will be bigger than the previous 50."

The Biggest Edge in the 21st Century

What accounts for the surging popularity of **referral marketing**? For one thing, the industry offers one-of-a-kind, cutting-edge products available exclusively through affiliate distributors. And certainly a big edge is the opportunity for average people to earn above-average incomes while helping others escape from jobs that pay too little money while demanding too much time.

Another big edge is "intellectual distribution," a phrase coined by Paul Zane Pilzer in his bestselling book *The Next Millionaires*. Because direct sellers take the time to educate consumers and answer questions about products that improve their lives, **referral marketing** holds a big edge over mass retailers, who are more interested in ringing up another sale than educating the consumer.

But in marketing, the **biggest edge**, as Burke Hedges calls it in his classic book *Who Stole the American Dream II?* is "face time," that irreplaceable, one-on-one, person-to-person, face-to-face interaction between one human being and another.

Biggest Edge of Referral Marketing

Big Edge	**Biggest Edge**
Cutting-edge products	Face-to-face contacts
Income opportunity	

As Burke writes, "In our increasingly cold, isolated hi-tech world, the **biggest edge** is a firm handshake... a warm smile... a confident demeanor... steady eye contact... active listening... a hearty laugh... a loving look... a pat on the back... a knowing nod... a hug of acceptance.

In our hi-tech, Brave New Wired World, the need for hi-touch contacts can never be digitized. And never replaced.

Give Yourself an Edge-up in the Global Economy

Millions of average people worldwide are making money... having fun... calling their own shots... setting their own hours... and living their own dreams by leveraging their **contact capital** with **referral marketing**.

Some people will take advantage of this opportunity.

Some people won't.

How about you?

Direct mail [more commonly called 'junk mail']
is, above all, the art and science of getting
people to act—and act immediately.

—*Alan Rosenspan*
direct marketing expert

7

How Others Are Making Cash on Your Contacts

Junk mail makes it easy to predict what you'll find in your mailbox each day: applications for credit cards and home equity loans… flyers and catalogs… magazine subscriptions… pizza coupons… postcards offering "guaranteed lowest rates" on car insurance, etc., etc.

We automatically toss out 99% of our junk mail without even opening it. But the other 1% meets some need and we act—we sign up for that low-rate credit card or call that discount auto insurance agency. (By the way, a 1% success rate isn't an exaggeration. According to the Direct Marketing Association, the average response rate has fallen from 2% to less that 1% today).

Warming Up to Cold Contacts

Now, you'd think successful businesses wouldn't be interested in investing their money in marketing campaigns that failed 99% of the time, would you?

But just the opposite is true—direct mail is on track to hit 120 billion units by 2008, making it 50% larger than all other mail combined. In 2007, direct mail advertising was surpassed only by TV and far outpaced advertising expenditures in newspapers and on the Internet.

The chart on the next page shows the growth curve of direct mail compared to other types of advertising:

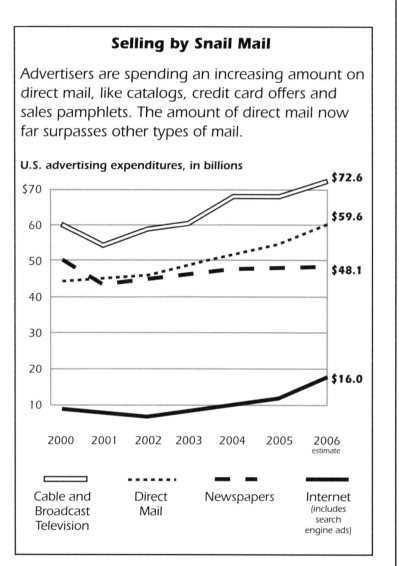

Selling by Snail Mail

Advertisers are spending an increasing amount on direct mail, like catalogs, credit card offers and sales pamphlets. The amount of direct mail now far surpasses other types of mail.

U.S. advertising expenditures, in billions

$72.6
$70
$59.6
60
50
$48.1
40
30
20
$16.0
10

2000 2001 2002 2003 2004 2005 2006
                                    estimate

Cable and   Direct   Newspapers   Internet
Broadcast   Mail   (includes
Television   search
                                             engine ads)

As you can see, the century-old marketing method known as direct mail has raced past newspaper advertising and is three times bigger than Internet ads, contradicting the experts' predictions that advertising on the "new media" will soon make marketing via the old media obsolete.

Someone forgot to tell advertisers that junk mail is dead.

Truth is, it's the fastest-growing conventional marketing medium.

Cold Contacts vs. Connected Contacts

Now, notice I said *conventional* marketing medium.

Yes, direct mail is the fastest-growing *conventional* method of sales and marketing, but, with its 1% response rate, its effectiveness pales in comparison to the *unconventional* method of **referral marketing,** also called affiliate marketing or network marketing.

The biggest edge for referral marketing is word-of-mouth recommendations, the oldest and most effective method of marketing ever invented. In a recent study by the market research firm Keller Fay Group, 50% of the respondents said they were "highly likely" to buy a product or service based on word of mouth.

Which means that word-of-mouth marketing, with its 50% positive response rate, is *50 times more effective than direct mail*, which averages 1%.

What accounts for the huge disparity? *The quality of the contacts.*

You see, direct mail relies on **cold contacts** for its leads, while the **referral marketing** concept relies on **connected contacts**. Let's take a moment to discuss this all-important difference.

Turning Cold Contacts into Cold, Hard Cash

Cold contacts are contacts in which the marketer has a customer history or a demographic interest in the target audience. Just think about all of the junk mail you receive—good chance you hadn't even heard of 90% of the companies before their literature started showing up in your mailbox.

So how did they get your name and address?

Simple—if you subscribed to a magazine... made a donation to a charity or political party... answered a survey... signed up for a product warranty... or bought a gift from a catalog, then you're on hundreds of lists that have been bought and sold countless times.

It's nearly impossible NOT to be on mailing lists. The largest mailing list in existence is simply a compilation of all of the names listed in more than 4,000 phone books across the U.S. and contains 210 *million* names.

Comparing Cold Contacts to Connected Contacts

Whereas **cold contacts** are mostly based on hi-tech *demographic* associations, **connected contacts** are based on hi-touch *social* associations, such as family, friends, co-workers, club members, church groups, etc. **Connected contacts** aren't just limited to people you know personally but include everyone connected to you by a common cause or commitment.

If you're a member of a local Rotary Club, for example, then your **connected contacts** include not only the club members in your local chapter but also the 1.2 million members in 32,000 clubs in more than 200 countries.

Connected contacts, by virtue of their hi-touch capacity, are far richer in **contact capital** than **cold contacts**—*50 times richer, in fact,* as evidenced by the 1% positive response for junk mail compared to a 50% positive response to person-to-person marketing.

The biggest disparity between **cold contacts** and **your contacts**, however, isn't the potential but the application. Direct mail is only 1/50th as effective as network marketing, yet your contacts are buying stuff from them on a regular basis.

Why?

Because direct mailers are asking your contacts for their business. And your contacts are buying from them.

Someone is making cash on your contacts, right? *Why not you? Why not now?*

You Can't Avoid Being Converted into Cashflow

We've established that your contacts are buying hundreds if not thousands of dollars of products and services each year from people they don't know and will never meet working for companies they have nothing in common with.

Places That Turn Your Contacts into Consumers

Direct mailers

Catalogs

Retailers

Discount Stores

Internet Sites

When people you know spend money at a discount store, an Internet site, a retailer, or a catalog, it means your contacts are being converted into someone's cashflow, isn't that true?

Wouldn't it make more sense for your contacts to buy products from you, a person they know and trust, than a giant chain store or Internet site interested only in their money?

Sure it would!

Who Gets Invited to Grand Openings? Friends? Or Strangers?

Connected contacts are the springboard for virtually every successful new business. If you were to open a new restaurant or retail store, for example, who would you make sure got on the guest list for the grand opening? Your neighbors, friends, and family members, right?

If you were starting a new business—whether it's in retail... real estate... insurance... financial planning... consulting... or even franchising—you'd be wise to advertise first to people you know, using your **connected contacts** to create much-needed momentum and, yes, cashflow. Assuming you offer great products and provide great service, your friends will recommend your business to their neighbors, friends, and family members, creating a self-sustaining customer base.

Inviting people you know to a grand opening isn't taking advantage of a friendship—it's the opposite—it's *honoring* a friendship by asking special people in your life to participate in a special occasion. Likewise, if you represent a product or service that will enrich and improve your friends' lives, do your friends a favor and give them the courtesy of sharing it with them! And then share how you can help them convert their **contact capital** into cashflow.

They'll not only get a product they need. They'll get a dream recharged.

What could be better than that?

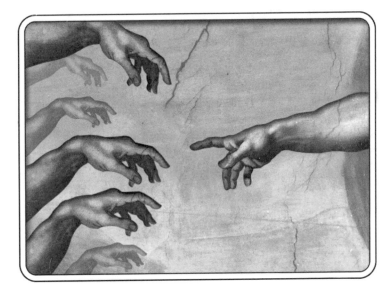

There are no strangers in this world—only friends I haven't met yet.

—*Will Rogers*

8

Endless Contacts

The much-discussed concept called **six degrees of separation** theorizes that everybody in the world is separated by just six social ties, meaning that any individual can contact any other individual in the world with just six phone calls or e-mails.

Sounds pretty far-fetched, doesn't it?

I mean, do you really think some random guy in, say, Moscow, Idaho, could get an e-mail routed to someone he has never met in Moscow, Russia, in six e-mails or fewer?

"Yes," says Duncan Watts, a professor at Columbia University, who conducted a study of 60,000 people from 166 different countries to test the **six degrees** theory. Participants were given the e-mail address of one of 18 different target people scattered around the globe and were instructed to contact that person by sending e-mails to people the participants knew and were likely "closer" to the target.

Sure enough, in most cases, it took between five and seven e-mails to contact a target.

Like the Disney song says, "It's a small world, after all."

Easier Than Ever to Facilitate Friendships

Social scientists cite Watts' experiment as further proof of interconnectedness and increasing **social capital** in the world. Indeed, easy access to e-mail, chat rooms, and social networking sites on the Internet, along with inexpensive cell phones and free long-distance service, have shrunk our world.

As a result, **social networks** can grow larger and span even greater distances, increasing not only the number of contacts but opening the possibility of transforming **cold contacts** into **connected contacts** by virtue of common bonds, as in, "I know, like, and trust Fred. And Fred knows, likes, and trusts Tom. So it's likely Tom and I should know, like, and trust each other."

Social networks—whether in the virtual world or the real world—offer shortcuts for expanding meaningful relationships with like-minded people. This doesn't mean, however, that

Facebook.com contacts can take the place of face-to-face contacts. Watts agrees:

> "In this [six degrees] experiment, the Internet is simply a tool we use to transmit messages," he said in an e-mail to *New Scientist*. "Compared to offline interactions like work, school, family, and community, I don't see e-mail as being a particularly compelling medium for generating social ties."

Hi-tech communication can never replace hi-touch contacts, but it can facilitate and speed up meaningful relationships. The dating site *eHarmony.com*, for example, uses detailed profiles to help single people find suitable mates. The first contact is cold via the Website, but people who connect can move to face-to-face meetings. It must be working—*eHarmony* boasts they are responsible for 90 marriages a day!

More Connected Contacts Than Ever Before

Expanded **social networks** have increased not only the quality of your **contact capital**, but also the quantity. More interconnectedness means access to more **connected contacts**.

**Expanded Social Networks
Mean More Connected Contacts**

More friends   More associates
More acquaintances
More co-workers   More business partners
More customers
More common causes
More common communities   More clients

Once you understand how to tap into **social networks,** you start planting the seeds for **endless contacts.** The key to **endless contacts** is to think of your contacts as **networks,** instead of single units. Thinking in terms of networks means your contacts BEGIN with a single person and expand to their contacts... and then expand again to the contacts of each of those contacts... and so on endlessly.

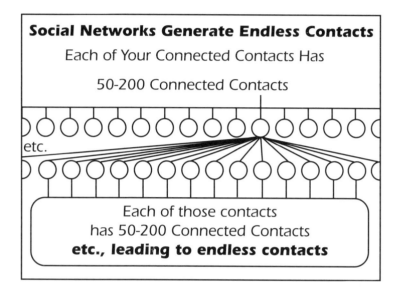

How to Make Their Contacts Your Contacts

If you ask your new distributors to make a list of contacts, each list will likely number 50 to 200 **connected contacts**— friends, family members, co-workers, acquaintances, neighbors, and so on.

Even if you don't know a single person on the list, by making three-way phone calls to each contact, you can transform a list of formerly **cold contacts** into a warm list of **connected contacts**. By cultivating relationships with individuals on someone else's list, you open the door to converting their contacts to your contacts, giving you **endless contacts**.

Next Step—Turning Contacts into Cashflow

The way to turn *contacts into cashflow*, then, is to work your list of contacts while teaching the contacts who join you in your business how to work *their* list of contacts... and then they, in turn, teach *their* new people how to work *their* list of contacts ... and so on, giving you **endless contacts** and creating a bigger cashflow.

Contacts are everywhere—your lists, your new distributors' lists, new acquaintances, chance meetings, introductions, clubs and organizations, etc. And each of these contacts has a social network of **connected contacts** just waiting to make a connection with you.

Those contacts are buying things they need and want from someone—most likely, someone they don't know and have no connection to.

Since they're buying those products anyway, why not buy them from you, while learning how to turn *their* **endless contacts**... into endless cashflow?

This one makes a net while that one stands and wishes. Would you like to make a bet which one gets the fishes?

Chinese children's rhyme

Your Actions Speak
So Loud I Can't Hear
What You're Saying

Can you correctly solve this simple riddle I first heard in elementary school?

Five birds are sitting on a telephone wire and three of them decide to fly away. How many birds are left sitting on the wire?

If your answer is "two," then you just joined the majority of respondents. But the majority is wrong.

The correct answer is "five."

Yes, three birds "decide" to fly away, but making a decision to fly is not the same as *acting* on that decision. A bird could make a decision to fly and still be sitting in the same spot two days later.

Get Going and Get Growing

You're likely reading this book because someone has shared an opportunity with you, or you have just *decided* to take advantage of **referral marketing** by joining a network marketing organization.

Congratulations for having an open mind. *Deciding* you liked what you saw and heard... and then *deciding* to join the business is an essential step toward turning contacts into cashflow.

Decisions are crucial for success.

But only *action* can turn your dreams into reality.

Decide... Then Do!

Your contacts are the reason North America enjoys one of the highest standards of living in the world. That's what makes our economy strong and vibrant—people buying and selling, producing and consuming.

Every day your contacts are buying products and services they want and need while recommending to their friends new products to try and opportunities to check out.

Somebody—actually, a whole bunch of somebodies—are making money on your contacts.

Growing their business on your contacts.

Growing their bank account on your contacts.

Living their dreams on your contacts.

Saving for retirement on your contacts.

That's **contact capital** in action. Only one problem. Your contacts are buying products and services from someone—*but unless you take action, it won't be from you*!

Don't you think it's time you turned your contacts into cashflow while showing your friends and neighbors how they can do the same? Whether you *decide* to get involved in Network Marketing or not... and whether you take *action* to turn your contacts into cashflow... rest assured that someone, somewhere, is going to turn *your* contacts into *their* cashflow.

Someone is making money on your **contact capital**.

Why not you?

Why not now?